**A New Way of Reading
the Classic Book of Wisdo**

reflections on the tao te ching

tao te
ching

David K. Reynolds, Ph.D.

William Morrow and Company, Inc.
New York

It is the policy of William Morrow and Company, Inc., and
its imprints and affiliates, recognizing the importance of
preserving what has been written, to print the books we
publish on acid-free paper, and we exert our best efforts to
that end.

Library of Congress Cataloging-in-Publication Data

Reynolds, David K.
    Reflections on the *tao te ching* : a new way of reading
the classic book of wisdom / by David K. Reynolds.
        p.   cm.
    Includes bibliographical references.
    ISBN 0-688-12258-2
    1. Lao-tzu. Tao te ching.   2. Life.   I. Title.
    BL1900.L35R49   1993   92-1665
    299'.51482—dc20   CIP

Printed in the United States of America

First Edition

1   2   3   4   5   6   7   8   9   10

BOOK DESIGN BY HARAKAWA SISCO

To Constructive Living instructors—

East and West

contents

Introduction

What I have written here is not a new translation of the *tao te ching*, but a work inspired by it. If some readers kindly consider these verses to contain accurate interpretations of the intent of the original work here and there then I shall be pleased, but such kindness would be only the equivalent of layering their interpretations on mine. The Chinese language is vague enough to permit numerous templates. Rather than describing Reality, our words are merely absorbed into it. Among the many fine translations of the *tao te ching*, I have benefited most from the Richard Wilhelm translation (rendered from the German into English by H. G. Ostwald), published in London by Arkana in 1985.

My reading of the *tao te ching* is based on a lifeway called Constructive Living. Constructive Living thought has roots deep in the history of the ancient East and branches into the psychological writings of Morita Masatake and Yoshimoto Ishin, Japanese thinkers and psychotherapists of this century. Constructive Living asks the student to pay attention to Reality, to be realistic and practical. It is unrealistic, for example, for the suffering student to attempt to control feelings directly by will. It is unrealistic to allow feelings to be the sole determinants of behavior. Unrealistic thinking is itself the modern term "neurosis."

Constructive Living holds that there are forms of suffering no one can escape, but that self-centeredness causes additional, unnecessary suffering. Constructive Living recommends losing oneself in one's circumstances. Rather than seeking to assure getting one's own share, the student of Constructive Living is advised to find the self by giving away narrow self-focus. Such thinking may sound familiar to those in the Taoist, Buddhist, Judeo-Christian, and Sufi traditions, to name a few.

Constructive Living is not a religion but an educational pursuit. However, there is the need to go beyond a mere intellectual grasp of the principles, to build life not on what one has read or heard but on what one has experienced. There is a naturalness to this lifeway. It is no oversight that Reality begins with a capital letter throughout the text.

PART ONE

transcendence of the ordinary

Where does Reality come from?

We talk, but no one knows—can know—

because knowing is already Reality.

Before knowing what was there?

With knowing comes detail.

What makes a miracle?

We don't understand.

Our knowing limits us.

There is only Reality.

That which we know; that which we don't know.

Source of miracles, secrets, everyday life.

Our minds create positive and negative, beautiful and ugly.

Meaning lies in opposition;

joy rests in pain and sorrow.

Hope springs from despair;

freedom emerges from obsession, needs obsession.

Neurotic moments define our respite;

they are ball and wall and rebound.

Thus are the colleagues of Constructive Living.

They dwell in just doing.

They teach by their actions.

When conditions arise

they act.

They are not obsessed with results.

They are effective in their disengagement.

When their task is complete

they move to the next task.

And Reality keeps emerging.

By accepting Reality

we quarrel neither with ourselves nor with others.

By releasing time and outcome

we are not possessed.

By avoiding wishful displays

we live straightforwardly.

The colleagues of Constructive Living

supplant theory with food,

rumination with action,

dreams with concrete plans.

They give away their wisdom freely.

Only doing, then next doing.

R eality keeps coming.

It is the source of everything,

the start of each moment.

It sharpens our vision.

It exercises our minds.

It tempers time.

It administers life and death.

It is beyond knowing, yet it is real.

It forms the ground for this moment's thought.

R eality just happens.

Humans are no more than part of it.

Don't stop for morality.

Participate in Reality.

Play yourself on Reality's flute.

Act on it;

learn from it.

Don't waste time with explanations.

Recognize and do.

T he Now keeps emerging.

It is the Great Giver.

It is opportunity.

It continues presenting itself—

Effectively.

A s we proceed with our creations of mind,

the world keeps arising.

It is a gift from Reality.

Thus also are the compatriots of Constructive Living.

Unlimited by concepts of character or personality

they expand by giving themselves away.

And thus save themselves.

What is ours?

All Reality is a gift.

We are "gifted."

8

W ater flows, changes.

It carries out its vocation well,

without complaint.

It considers itself to be nothing special.

By its movement it reveals its source and destination.

Proper attitude,

apt giving,

rightful speech,

appropriate discipline,

befitting work,

suitable, timely action.

Reality's representative—

deriving neither praise nor blame.

Reality changes, flows.

It cannot be stopped, held.

We cannot stop time with possessions or name.

Foolish, blind attempts.

Just doing: not *me* doing, not *my* doing.

Can you focus totally on the task at hand?

Can you see and hear and touch your surroundings

with an open mind?

Can you disregard your own convenience?

Can you feel and act naturally

without obsessing with oughts and shoulds?

Whatever change occurs

without flying away

can you sit on the eggs of Reality?

Can you see clearly enough to know

when nonaction is action?

Just offering,

however accepted.

Just growing vast

while growing small.

Just doing Reality's work.

Recognized or not.

The less self, the better.

The more emptiness, the more to take in.

The more openness, the fresher the air.

Filled with self, we stumble.

However much we own

Emptiness offers capacity.

The ads blind us.

Commercials deafen us.

Rich foods clog us.

We strive so hard

for the Good Life.

Sensible folks

take care of their bodies.

Just *this* is plenty.

When we achieve our goal

we fear to lose it.

When we achieve eminence

we fear exposure.

What is mine?

What have I alone achieved?

Whoever is the world

owns the world.

Whoever accepts the world

receives the world.

From where does Reality emanate?

From where does each fresh moment emerge?

From where do thoughts appear?

This source is inexplicable.

Welling up, replaced, disappearing.

Welling up, disappearing.

Welling up.

It is the continuous thread of arising Reality.

We cannot know the thoughts of others.

We cannot know the past.

We know only the surface, now.

We assign qualities to past people and events.

Take it all in.

Time passes.

Know just this much, here.

It is enough.

Reality keeps coming.

Thoughts keep rising from nowhere,

returning to nowhere.

Nowhere appears still, fate-full.

Nowhere has no time boundaries.

Events have long-term implications.

Just wait.

Heaven is acceptance of what is.

Acceptance leads to action.

Action leads to more Reality.

Whatever happens, Reality emerges.

It's not me who rules this life.

Self-praise, self-love, self-fear, self-contempt

are ephemeral.

Words create a pseudo-reality.

Do and results follow.

You become free!

Rules are no substitute

for wisdom.

Scholarly theories are no substitute

for truth.

Social morals are no substitute

for clarity.

Some cling to laws, cling to people.

Reality alone is valid.

Religion and scholarship create

artificial validity.

Civic laws create

artificial morality.

Advertising creates

artificial desires.

Undermine this attractive artificiality.

Demonstrate the simplicity of Reality.

Self-centeredness causes suffering.

Give it up

in exchange for freedom.

Words here

Words there.

Feelings fade

while we act.

All of us doing;

Shining doing.

Sometimes hesitant,

sometimes fretful,

sometimes unsettled.

Forgetting the bounty of Reality.

Confused by cleverness.

Self-focused.

Purpose forgotten

Isolated by rumination.

Notice! Notice!

R eality is all there is.

We view through darkened glass.

We obscure its images.

Yet it holds the seed of truth.

Reality is constant, reliable.

Yet we keep assigning smudged labels

to our file folders of life.

Reality keeps changing;

so do the colleagues of Constructive Living.

They are recognized for their flexibility.

They give themselves away to gain everything.

They empty themselves to admit all of Reality.

They focus on their purpose and act, imperfectly.

They accept Reality as it is.

And do their share to affect it.

23

Words can confuse.

They fall lightly and dissolve.

They are used to point to eons.

They generate more words.

Unchanging words, changing Reality.

Where is your allegiance?

Set yourself to live realistically

with those who live realistically

in Reality.

Fit yourself to Reality's circumstances.

You will recognize the others.

They will recognize you.

No faith, no belief,

Only recognition.

Don't try to push time and space.

Don't aim for perfection.

Just be your true self,

your imperfect self.

Pride is tasteless ignorance.

Opposed to all things.

Unrealistic.

In the beginning was the Word

But It was not a word.

What to call It?

So unlike any-thing,

so incomparable.

Yet It is everything we know.

Continuing, continuous, all.

Let's call It Reality.

Cheating, I call it vast, changing, intimate, wonderful.

That fog and this poppy partake of its wonder.

We partake of its wonder.

Nested in Reality.

Reality nests in Itself.

Qualities contain their opposites.

So do we, colleagues of Constructive Living.

We live each day with our contradictions.

We accept them.

We take responsibility for them.

We aren't tied down

by notions of personality.

Minimal clutter for others to clean up.

Minimal chatter for others to dispute.

Minimal dependence on things.

Minimal defensiveness.

Minimal aggressiveness.

Constructive Living is self-evident,

there is no need to force it on others.

Nothing is unworthy;

give all things new life.

Exemplary living models these lessons.

Others watch with eager eyes.

This debt to our teachers,

This action-love of our lifeway

puts us beyond scholarship.

28

S ometimes this, sometimes that,

living in this moment,

we are children.

Holding to purpose,

recognizing our limits,

we trek the eternal Now.

Newly created over and over.

Like it or not

we are lived.

In acknowledgment lies depth.

Thank you.

Thank you.

Just this.

Just doing what needs doing.

Constructive Living people

govern themselves.

So each moment brings its tasks.

We can't push Reality around.

Reality has a Mind of its own.

Lean against it, it evaporates.

Grasp it, it vanishes.

Ever shifting.

The modest colleagues of Constructive Living

Avoid

Intemperate demands on Reality.

W **e outfit the advice**

we offer the world.

What we give out returns to us.

Direct opposition produces frustration and exhaustion.

Work toward your purpose.

Feelings can't be forced.

Lean on your purpose.

Accomplish your goal without boasting

simply because it needed to be.

Hurting anything has no value.

We hurt by hurting.

Showing off our power is foolish.

Threatening is the tactic of the feeble.

But use strength when necessary.

We prefer peace and quiet.

Victory implies defeat.

Who would rejoice in the downfall of others?

They are me.

Their deaths produce my funeral.

32

What is simpler than this moment?

Yet we cannot control its appearance or passing.

No president or dictator governs it.

We use words in our attempt to bind it.

But words merely symbolize Reality.

They emerge into Reality only as words.

Don't believe them.

Words are tiny representatives of vast Reality.

S tudy others to become skillful.

Study yourself to become wise.

What else is there to study?

Act on others to have influence.

Act on yourself to have strength.

Expressing your needs is one thing.

Working to achieve them is quite another.

Don't be distracted from your purpose.

Don't lose yourself in rumination.

R eality is everywhere,

giving existence to everything.

Reality owns nothing.

It nurtures all things.

It dominates nothing.

Humbly it presents the world to our senses.

How dependent we are on its largess!

Constructive Living peers are like that.

They quietly go about their business.

D on't lose sight of the Mystery.

The world comes to learn of it,

and finds truth,

not disappointment.

Constructive Living isn't flashy.

It's plain.

It doesn't appear to be precious.

It doesn't sound special.

Put it into action

and discover its marvelous depths.

Stop trying to wrap up your feelings into a neat package.

Feel what you feel.

Let your feelings flourish.

What real choice have you?

Be clear on this point,

and get on with your life of doing.

When is "not doing," doing?

When does "leaving untouched" produce change?

Attention to one's tasks

minimizes focus on unpleasant feelings.

Keep your priorities straight.

Reality must be accepted as it is

in order to savor it.

Those who try to own Reality

cannot taste its true flavor.

Reality cannot be pushed or forced.

Deduce right and wrong from attention to Reality.

Create a system of justice in the same way.

Grasp the essence of love and appreciation similarly.

If the observation of Reality is lost,

all is lost.

Don't build your life solely on what Reality might bring.

Build your life on what is solid and real.

Hold to Reality.

Reality holds all things.

It is the way things are.

Ifs are only if-Reality.

We all come from It.

It sustains us.

Dependable Reality.

Yield to Reality's spiral.

We owe it our existence.

Where did Reality come from?

The wise take Reality seriously.

The clever want to discuss their doubts.

The foolish think Reality is foolish,

Or ignore it as best they can.

Don't depend on superficial appearances.

Concepts can confuse.

Reality keeps on giving,

fulfilling its promises.

F irst there is Reality

Then there is me thinking about Reality.

Then there is me thinking about me thinking about Reality.

The mind creates "things."

Yet all things spring from Reality.

They fit together, thanks to Reality.

We loathe despair, loneliness, insignificance.

Yet we all experience these feelings.

In trying to suppress them

we exaggerate them.

In embracing them

we diminish them.

This teaching is not new.

The stronger our desires

the greater we fear failure.

We die a thousand unnatural deaths

unnecessarily.

Our desires push us around.

Our anticipatory anxiety

interferes with current action,

Though it need not.

Acting on impulse,

acting from feelings alone,

what benefit is there?

Few understand when not-doing is doing.

The name or the person,

which is more real?

People or things,

which is more valuable?

Success or failure,

just words.

We add judgment to Reality

and seek after mind-text.

Missing the details.

Accumulating possessions

we miss nonpossessable Reality.

Reality-esteem is trustworthy.

Self-esteem is not.

Avoid the dangers inherent in asserting self.

Just this moment's task is sufficient.

Completion never occurs.

Imperfect, tottering steps.

Witlessly press on.

It's good enough.

Give new life to people and things.

Use well what there is to use.

We want so much.

We bemoan what we have.

In the discrepancy lies discontent.

R eality is right here in front of you.

What has it brought you to do?

The farther you go

the less you have to figure out.

The colleague of Constructive Living

need not run about busily,

or understand everything,

or see with perfect clarity.

Complete in this, here, now.

Academic knowledge is increasingly complex.

Constructive lives are increasingly simple.

Simplify your life naturally.

Just doing what is necessary.

Just enough time to do what needs doing.

Moment *for* moment

without obsessive activity.

Constructive Living compatriots adopt

the minds of others.

Fitting themselves to

mind-moments of goodness and trust.

Offering such moments to others.

The people of Constructive Living live quietly.

Others seek them out for their offerings

of surprisingly meaningful words.

We are all humans.

No one walks on air.

50

Paying attention to your surroundings *is* Life.

Ruminating *is* Death.

Some live often and well.

Some die often and needlessly.

There is freedom in this lifeway.

No handles for those who would control us.

No target for those who would hurt us.

No lack for those who would sell to us.

Receiving all in vulnerability.

What next?

R eality keeps on generating itself.

It provides us with experience.

It molds us.

It guides our everyday lives.

Nothing ignores Reality.

All things strive for life,

naturally.

So Reality creates us all,

over and over again.

It protects us

and brings us to completion.

Discover the roots of thoughts

to find the roots of this world.

Then you will be solidly grounded.

You cannot put your affairs in order

by talking about them.

Pay attention to detail.

Build strength on experiential understanding.

Study Constructive Living to remind yourself

of these truths.

But living constructively is not the whole of it.

To live fully in Reality

is to avoid obsession and compulsion.

In the midst of materialistic plenty,

in the midst of empty life-styles,

in the midst of meaningless glamour,

lies directionless activity.

You cannot be uprooted from this lifeway.

You won't fall away from Constructive Living.

Build a past,

build a self,

build a connection,

build a breadth

into life.

Make judgments on the basis of your own experience.

Evaluate people and countries and the world

as you evaluate yourself.

How do I know these truths?

From experience.

55

When you understand the fullness of Reality,

everything is interesting.

Distractions and boredom go away.

Uncertain, you go forward.

Richly endowed with feeling.

You never tire of Reality's presentation.

Partaking of Reality's timelessness.

Coming from no-time into time.

Presenting itself clearly to us.

To broaden one's awareness brings satisfaction.

To master self-discipline brings rewards.

Gather realistic experience.

For experience prepares you for death.

56

How can experience be expressed in words?

Attention is distracted by talking.

Be still and attend.

Suppress the quick retort.

Let agitation still itself with time.

Don't act wise.

Be ordinary.

Develop a bond with ordinary Reality,

and so accept extremes.

Love comes and goes.

Profits come and go.

Fame comes and goes.

Discover the wonder of the ordinary.

You can develop skills

to manage, to compete.

But in order to win the game of life

you must stop straining and start noticing.

Such is the way life is.

The more rules you give yourself

the narrower you become.

The more you attack

the more you are destroyed.

The more you trust intellect alone

the more trouble you create.

The deeper you look at yourself

the more imperfection you find.

So wise guides advise:

Don't aim to perfect yourself.

Don't rush into changing yourself.

Just do what needs doing

while accepting your feelings.

58

The mind that runs inconspicuously

causes least trouble.

The mind that governs strictly

produces deception and discord.

Sometimes happy, sometimes not.

The natural response to each situation

is best.

Turning Reality into projection

actuality into imagination

we generate unnecessary misery.

So are the comrades of Constructive Living.

They go about their lives straightforwardly,

and become models for others.

They yield to Reality without untimely suffering.

They earnestly hold to their purposes.

They shine without gloss.

Recognize Reality's genuine limits.

Avoid from the start

wasting time

on the truly impossible.

Use fully what is usable.

Rise to every occasion

and own all of Reality.

Everything is here, now.

Eternity is here, now.

Don't lose it.

E xercise your mind carefully,

as though writing a check.

When we apply these principles to life

our pasts don't haunt us.

And we don't attack faded cardboard cutouts.

Past and present work to support us.

Many streams flow into Constructive Living's lake.

Noticed or not,

reflecting clear depths of Reality.

Absorbing, absorbed.

Just ordinary water

quenching the thirst of some beings.

F rom Reality springs everything.

Mirroring pleasant and unpleasant thoughts.

Praising, condemning.

No need to fling off sorrow, depression.

We rule our actions.

Kneel to Reality

and go on about life.

In action lies hope.

In action lies reprieve.

How marvelous to have this prospect!

W hoever practices acceptance

accepts self as is,

creates meaning

ascribes value

repays Reality.

Only this step, now.

Only this effort, here.

Beginnings start now.

Beginnings start here.

Think of the ultimate deed,

and today's deed is undone.

Overwhelmed by potential,

today's talent isn't actualized.

Cavalier or compulsive—

muddled maps for losing your way.

Plan ahead, but act forthrightly.

64

It's not so difficult to grasp the way things are.

We can anticipate all sorts of possibilities.

We can generate and demolish dreams in a flash.

We can distract ourselves in many ways.

Even before the whole picture emerges

we can work on this small part.

Actions accumulate.

Behavior makes changes.

There is no security.

Constructive people

act sensibly,

without fixation.

Do everything with full attention

from beginning to end.

The people of Constructive Living

aren't preoccupied by desires.

They stop yearning for the impossible.

They value experiential understanding.

They return to solid realism,

naturally.

Their actions aren't forced.

To teach Reality.

one must teach minimally.

Dependence on the intellect alone

leads to trouble.

Know the value of experience.

Discover yourself in Reality.

Be prepared for surprises,

immensity,

attainment.

H umility is realistic,

and triumphant.

Just be where you are,

rightfully.

Work on your debts.

Minimize your vexation of others.

The world keeps giving,

willingly.

The world keeps sustaining,

without quarrel.

This course appears interesting to some

but useless.

It is, in a sense, useless.

It is no more than talk about

the way things are.

Curing neurosis alone would diminish it.

These treasures are worth the search:

compassionate action,

self-determined action,

informed action.

Pushing ahead without such action is futile

even in struggle.

Reality offers us the model of compassion.

Don't let feelings govern your life.

Avoid quarreling; do low status.

Be unobtrusive, like Reality.

Keep your senses sharp.

Don't press Reality.

Notice that purposes arise.

Act as Reality's representative.

Do what needs doing

however difficult or painful.

Or lose your foothold.

No need to feel good about it.

Constructive Living is easy to understand

and readily turned into action.

But few understand,

and few evince the action.

Where do words come from?

Where does action come from?

That source is not understood.

So Constructive Living is misunderstood.

My task is to point to the misunderstanding.

This path appears unexceptional,

concealing the extraordinary.

E xperiential understanding is precious.

To disregard it causes suffering.

When you suffer enough, you may return.

And rediscover Reality.

So sufficient suffering may reduce suffering.

Be afraid of what is fearful.

Be as vast as your world.

Constriction produces distress.

Constriction is distress.

Thus are the people of Constructive Living.

They realistically view themselves as nothing special.

They recognize Reality's magnificence,

and eschew the insignificant.

They give up unreality for living in the Now.

Unnecessary risk-taking is childish.

Doing courage promotes life.

Why is it thus?

Constructive Living compatriots

perceive the simplicity and the complexity.

And they yield to Reality.

Noticing alternatives,

embracing resistance,

planning, waiting, acting.

All part of Reality's events.

Sometimes terrified, sometimes not.

We cannot conquer our fear of death

by killing it.

But fear of death can kill us.

We can kill ourselves through fear

before death does.

Death in life is painful.

H ead in the clouds,

you trip over your feet.

Cerebration, speculation, rumination

may make action difficult.

You will die.

Use time well.

Don't wait for the grand life accomplishment.

Just this deed, now.

F **lexibility overcomes rigidity.**

Fresh awareness fills in life's furrows.

Obsession and compulsion are not lifelike.

Open vulnerability is vital.

Attack your feelings and lose to them.

Give in to Reality

and win.

Aim for a balanced life.

Reduce your feeling-focus.

Increase your action-focus.

And so round out your life.

Too many people sacrifice behavior

in the service of feelings.

Notice the feelings,

and give them away to the world.

So are the people of Constructive Living.

They act without being ensnared by results.

They move from deed to deed.

They know that their accomplishments

are not *their* accomplishments.

Water is frail and feeble.

Yet it gets its water work done.

It moves toward its goal.

Just being water.

You know its power.

Just be water.

You can't work on your feelings.

You needn't work on them.

What is the point of it?

Just do what Reality presents.

Be responsible for yourself.

Those who live fully

behave with personal responsibility.

Those who lack Life

demand more from Reality.

Don't strive for perfection.

Work at the substantial and authentic.

All you have is you; that is sufficient.

Don't stray from your purposes;

someday you will die.

Don't trust in technique.

Don't trust in technology.

Grace and works are one.

Live gracefully

with your eyes on your surroundings

and your feet headed straight.

81

The truth is plain truth.

Fancy words are not true.

Persuasion is unnecessary,

whether from argument or even skill.

High scholarship is unnecessary—

neither courses nor degrees.

The people of Constructive Living

don't fixate on unpossessed possessions.

What they possess they give away.

And so possess more.

Fulfillment lies in moving attentively.

Fulfillment lies in accepting the Whole

while doing our Part.

Books

Reynolds, David K. *A Thousand Waves.* New York: Morrow, 1990.

Reynolds, David K. *Constructive Living.* Honolulu: University of Hawaii Press, 1984.

Reynolds, David K. *Constructive Living for Young People.* Tokyo: Asahi, 1988.

Reynolds, David K. *Even in Summer the Ice Doesn't Melt.* New York: Morrow, 1986.

Reynolds, David K. *The Heart of the Japanese People.* Tokyo: Nichieisha, 1980.

Reynolds, David K. *Living Lessons.* Tokyo: Asahi Shuppansha, 1984.

Reynolds, David K. *Modern Aesop's Fables.* Tokyo: Nichieisha, 1984.

Reynolds, David K. *Morita Psychotherapy* (English, Japanese, and Spanish editions). Berkeley: University of California Press, 1976.

Reynolds, David K. *Naikan Psychotherapy: Meditation for Self-Development.* Chicago: University of Chicago Press, 1983.

Reynolds, David K. *Playing Ball on Running Water.* New York: Morrow, 1984.

Reynolds, David K. *Pools of Lodging for the Moon.* New York: Morrow, 1989.

Reynolds, David K. *The Quiet Therapies.* Honolulu: University of Hawaii Press, 1980.

Reynolds, David K. *Rainbow Rising from a Stream.* New York: Morrow, 1992.

Reynolds, David K. *Thirsty, Swimming in the Lake.* New York: Morrow, 1991.

Reynolds, David K. *Water Bears No Scars.* New York: Morrow, 1987.

Reynolds, David K. *Winning the Game of Life.* Tokyo: Asahi, 1988.

Reynolds, David K., ed. *Flowing Bridges, Quiet Waters.* Albany, N.Y.: SUNY Press, 1989.

Reynolds, David K., ed. *Plunging Through the Clouds.* Albany, N.Y.: SUNY Press, 1992.

Book Chapters

Reynolds, David K. "Japanese Models of Psychotherapy." In *Health, Illness, and Medical Care in Japan,* eds. E. Norbeck and M. Lock. Honolulu: University of Hawaii Press, 1987.

Reynolds, David K. "Morita Psychotherapy." In *Handbook of Innovative Psychotherapies,* ed. R. Corsini. New York: Wiley, 1981.

Reynolds, David K. "Morita Therapy in America." In *Modern Morita Therapy,* eds.

T. Kora and K. Ohara. Tokyo: Hakuyosha, 1977.

Reynolds, David K. "Morita Therapy in America." In *Morita Therapy: Theory and Practice,* ed. K. Ohara. Tokyo: Kongen, 1987 (in Japanese).

Reynolds, David K. "Naikan Therapy." In *Handbook of Innovative Psychotherapies,* ed. R. Corsini, New York: Wiley, 1981.

Reynolds, David K. "On Being Natural: Two Japanese Approaches to Healing." In *Eastern and Western Approaches to Healing,* eds. A. A. Sheikh and K. S. Sheikh. New York: Wiley, 1989.

Reynolds, David K. "Psychocultural Perspectives on Death." In *Living and Dying with Cancer,* ed. P. Ahmed. New York: Elsevier, 1981.

Articles

Reynolds, David K. "Meaningful life therapy." *Culture, Medicine and Psychiatry,* 3, 457–63, 1989.

Reynolds, David K. "Morita therapy and reality centered living." *International Bulletin of Morita Therapy,* 1(1), 35, 1988.

Reynolds, David K. "Naikan therapy: an experiential view." *International Journal of Social Psychiatry,* 23(4), 252–64, 1977.

Reynolds, David K. "Psychodynamic insight and Morita psychotherapy." *Japanese Journal of Psychotherapy Research,* 5(4), 58–60, 1979.

Reynolds, David K., and C. W. Kiefer. "Cultural adaptability as an attribute of therapies: the case of Morita psychotherapy." *Culture, Medicine, and Psychiatry,* , 395–412, 1977.

Reynolds, David K., and Radmila Moacanin. "Eastern therapy: Western patient." *Japanese Journal of Psychotherapy Research,* 3, 305–16, 1976.

Reynolds, David K., and Joe Yamamoto. "Morita psychotherapy in Japan." In ed. Jules Masserman. *Current Psychiatric Therapies,* 13, 219–27, 1973.

Tapes

Krech, Gregg. *Doing a Good Job.* Arlington, Virginia: ToDo Institute, 1989.

Krech, Gregg. *Naikan.* Arlington, Virginia: ToDo Institute, 1990.

Reynolds, David K. *Doing What Needs to Be Done.* San Francisco: New Dimensions Foundation, 1990.

Reynolds, David K. *The Mountain Flows; The River Sits.* Arlington, Virginia: ToDo Institute, 1989.

Reynolds, David K. *The Sound of Rippling Water.* Arlington, Virginia: ToDo Institute, 1987.

APPENDIX

For information about the nearest Constructive Living instruction and Constructive Living group programs, call:

New York State	(914) 255-3918
New York City	(212) 472-7925
Washington, D.C.	(301) 530-5356
Los Angeles	(213) 389-4088
Chicago	(708) 234-9394
Cleveland	(216) 321-0442
San Francisco	(415) 584-0626

or contact Dr. Reynolds:

Constructive Living
P.O. Box 85
Coos Bay, Oregon 97420
(503) 269-5591

Available from William Morrow/Quill

Rainbow Rising from a Stream: The Natural Way to Well-Being

David K. Reynolds, Ph.D.
Dr. David K. Reynolds provides a brilliantly simple and effective way to na
igate life—through Constructive Living, a straightforward and pragmatic wa
of living.
0-688-11967-0

Thirsty, Swimming in the Lake: Essentials of Constructive Living

David K. Reynolds, Ph.D.
The leading authority on Morita therapy shows how to overcome commo
neuroses such as procrastination, phobias, addictions, and carelessnes
Koans, exercises, maxims, case histories, and parables show how life ca
be lived meaningfully with full attention to doing what needs to be done.
0-688-11032-0

A Thousand Waves: A Sensible Life-Style for Sensitive People

David K. Reynolds, Ph.D.
"Trying to subdue a wave by striking it only results in a thousand waves
(Morita Masatake). As we try to suppress one feeling, such as shyness o
anxiety, we succeed only in generating a thousand others. *A Thousand Wave*
is a comprehensive guide to Morita and Naikan, the Japanese ways to mor
positive living.
0-688-09434-1

Pools of Lodging for the Moon: Strategies for a Positive Life-Style

David K. Reynolds, Ph.D.
Through case histories of students, exercises, Zen koans, and instructiv
fables, Dr. Reynolds shows how to meet the fresh challenges that life bring
and how to practice the art of living well from moment to moment.
0-688-11278-1

Water Bears No Scars

David K. Reynolds, Ph.D.
This is David K. Reynolds's third volume of instruction in the Morita lifeway, the Japanese way to a more constructive, action-based life.
0-688-07448-0

Even in Summer the Ice Doesn't Melt

David K. Reynolds, Ph.D.
Presents the Japanese road to learning to live more constructively and responsibly, written by the leading Western authority on Morita therapy.
0-688-06744-1

Playing Ball on Running Water

David K. Reynolds, Ph.D.
The first popular introduction to a proven Japanese method for helping people reach beyond depression and neurosis to a life of action and accomplishment.
0-688-03913-8